LIFE CYCLES

The Emperor Penguin

Diana Noonan

CHELSEA
CLUBHOUSE

An Imprint of Chelsea House Publishers
A Haights Cross Communications Company
Philadelphia

Chelsea Clubhouse
1974 Sproul Road, Suite 400
Broomall, PA 19008-0914

The Chelsea House world wide web address is www.chelseahouse.com

Library of Congress Cataloging-in-Publication Data

Noonan, Diana.
    The emperor penguin / by Diana Noonan.
    p. cm. — (Life cycles)
    Summary: An introduction to the physical characteristics, behavior, and development from egg to adult of emperor penguins, birds that live in Antarctica.
    ISBN 0-7910-6965-6
    1. Emperor penguin—Life cycles—Juvenile literature. [1. Emperor penguin. 2. Penguins.] I. Title. II. Series.
QL696.S473 N66 2003
    598.47—dc21

                                                                                    2002000030

First published in 1999 by
MACMILLAN EDUCATION AUSTRALIA PTY LTD
627 Chapel Street, South Yarra, Australia, 3141

Copyright © Diana Noonan 1999
Copyright in photographs © individual photographers as credited

Edited by Anne McKenna
Text design by Polar Design
Cover design by Linda Forss

Printed in China

Acknowledgements

Cover: Emperor penguins in Antarctica with egg and chick. (Auscape © Graham Robertson)

Alan Parker, p. 24; Antarctic Division, Kingston, Tasmania, p. 14 © Rod Ledinham; A.N.T. Photo Library, pp. 5, 25, 30 © Jonathon Chester, 7, 20, 29 © Colin Blobel, 13, 22, 30 © M. Price, 21 © John Hoelscher; Auscape, pp. 4, 6, 8, 10, 12, 15, 16, 17, 18, 23, 30 © Graham Robertson, 9 © Michael Whitehead, 26 © Stefano Nicolini, 27 © Doug Allen–OSF; Australian Picture Library, p. 11 © ZEFA; Getty Images, p. 28.

While every care has been taken to trace and acknowledge copyright, the publisher tenders their apologies for any accidental infringement where copyright has proved untraceable.

Contents

Life Cycles

All animals change as they live and grow. They begin life as tiny creatures. They grow into adults that will produce their own young. The emperor penguin has its own special life cycle.

Emperor Penguins Are Birds

Emperor penguins are birds. They live in Antarctica on the ice and in the freezing-cold sea.

Birds are warm-blooded animals. Their body temperature stays the same. It does not matter how warm or cold the air or water is around them. Female birds lay eggs.

Emperor penguins hold their eggs on their feet.

Keeping Warm and Dry

Emperor penguins have feathers, but they cannot fly. Their oily feathers are waterproof to help keep their skin dry. They also have blubber. This thick layer of fat under the skin helps to keep the penguins warm.

Food

Emperor penguins hunt in the sea for squid and fish. They also eat tiny sea animals called krill. Emperors grow fatter and fatter during the summer months.

Winter

In winter most Antarctic birds and sea **mammals** go north to warmer places. Emperor penguins go south. The weather is even colder there. They waddle and skate on their bellies for long distances across the ice.

The Meeting Place

Emperor penguins meet at the nesting **colony** where they hatched as chicks. Thousands of emperor penguins gather together.

Emperor penguins gather at nesting colonies.

An emperor penguin calls to its mate.

At this time, the temperature is about minus 47 degrees Fahrenheit (minus 44 degrees Celsius). The penguins call to their mates. Emperor penguins seek out the same mate each year.

Courting and Mating

Emperor penguins **court**. They show off to each other. They sway and bow and pose. After a few days, they **mate**.

These emperor penguins are bowing to each other.

Laying Eggs

Soon the female emperor penguin lays one green-white egg. She pushes the egg onto her mate's feet with her beak. Then she goes back to the sea to hunt for food.

An emperor penguin does not have a real nest. The male keeps the egg on his feet. He covers the egg with a layer of blubber called a brood pouch. It keeps the egg warm.

brood pouch

Incubation

The male **incubates** the egg for 66 days. He keeps the egg safe and warm. The male stands for all this time. Male penguins **huddle** together to keep warm as the weather grows colder.

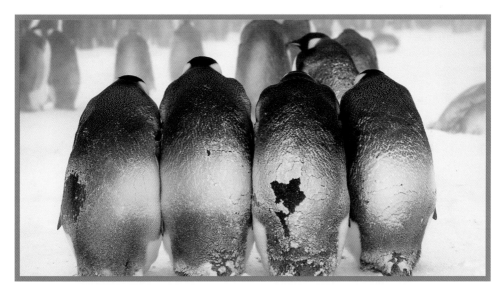

These emperor penguins are in a blizzard. They will huddle closer together as it gets colder.

The males move about with their eggs on their feet. They take turns standing on the cold outside edge of the group.

The male emperor penguin incubates the egg for more than two months. He goes without food for all this time. He grows thinner and thinner.

Hatching

Now the eggs are ready to hatch. The female emperors return to their mates. They have grown fat from feeding in the sea.

Female emperor penguins return to the colony.

The female's stomach is full of food for her newly hatched chicks. The male's stomach is empty. But he does have a little milky food left in his **crop** for the chicks.

Changing Guard

The male penguin shuffles the chick onto his mate's feet. Then he goes to sea to hunt for food.

This adult is feeding its chick.

The female **regurgitates** food for the chick for about three weeks. Then her mate comes back from the sea. The parents take turns hunting for food and caring for the chick.

Chicks

Emperor penguin chicks are fat and fluffy. But they still need their parents to help keep them warm. A chick stays under its parent's brood pouch for about six weeks.

Emperor penguin chicks stay together in a creche.

The chicks soon become too big for the brood pouch. They huddle together in a **creche**. Both parents then go to sea at the same time to hunt for food.

The weather grows warmer and the ice around the nesting site begins to melt. Penguin parents look for a hole in the ice. They can dive through the hole to hunt in the water. Then they do not need to make the long walk across the ice to the open sea.

This emperor penguin is walking back to the sea.

Molting

The chicks weigh about 22 pounds (10 kilograms) when they are 5 months old. They begin to **molt**, or lose their fluffy **down**. Down keeps the chicks warm while they are on the ice. Waterproof feathers grow in place of the down. The feathers will keep the chicks warm when they swim in the icy sea.

down

Emperor penguin chicks lose their down.

Chicks Alone

The parents leave the emperor chicks. The chicks must then look after themselves.

These chicks are going to sea for the first time.

Leopard seals hunt penguins.

The chicks must learn to swim, dive, and hunt for food. While young, they are in danger from other animals. Leopard seals and killer whales are some of the **predators** that hunt and eat young penguins.

Young Adult Emperors

Young emperors do not choose a mate until they are 4 to 6 years old. But they go back to visit their old colony before that time.

Chicks that grow into adults can live for
20 to 30 years. They go back to the same
colony each year. There they raise their
chicks in the coldest place in the world.

The Life Cycle of an Emperor Penguin

adults in nesting colony

egg under
brood pouch

going to sea

chick under
brood pouch

chicks molting

Glossary

colony   a gathering place for breeding animals

court   to try to attract a mate

creche   a group of young animals

crop   a place in the penguin's body where food is held so that it can be digested

down   a layer of fine, soft feathers

huddle   to stand in a closely packed group

incubate   to keep an egg warm for a period of time while it develops

mammal   a warm-blooded animal; female mammals give birth to live young; the young drink milk from the mother's body.

mate   to join with a breeding partner to produce young

molt   to shed; a penguin's down falls out when it molts; feathers replace the down.

predator   an animal that hunts other animals for food

regurgitate   to bring up food from the stomach to the mouth

Index